Published by Barbour Publishing, Inc., P.O. Box 719, Uhrichsville, Ohio 44683, www.barbourbooks.com

Our mission is to publish and distribute inspirational products offering exceptional value and biblical encouragement to the masses.

Printed in China.
5 4 3 2 1

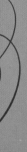

Christmas brings JOY to every heart!

Janice Clark

DayMaker
GREETING BOOKS

Christmas brings joy to every heart,
Sets old and young rejoicing,
What angels sang once to all on earth,
Oh, hear the children voicing.

Bright is the tree with lights aglow,
Like birds that perch together,
The child that holdeth Christmas dear
Shall keep these joys forever.

Joy comes to all the world today,
To halls and cottage hasting,
Come, sparrow and dove, from roof tree tall,
And share our Christmas feasting.

BERNHARDT S. INGEMANN, 1840
Translated from Danish by Cecil Cowdrey

So Joseph also went up from the town of Nazareth in Galilee to Judea, to Bethlehem the town of David, because he belonged to the house and line of David. He went there to register with Mary, who was pledged to be married to him and was expecting a child. While they were there, the time came for the baby to be born, and she gave birth to her firstborn, a son. She wrapped him in cloths and placed him in a manger, because there was no room for them in the inn.

LUKE 2:4–7

He came to us as a child,
and it is as children that we receive Him.
At least once in the year—if only for a moment—
we shed our adult shells and open our eyes and our hearts
to the miracle that is Christmas.

All My Heart This Night Rejoices

All my heart this night rejoices,
As I hear, far and near, sweetest angel voices;
"Christ is born," their choirs are singing,
Till the air, everywhere, now their joy is ringing.

PAUL GERHARDT, *PRAXIS PIETATIS MELICA* (1656)
TRANSLATED FROM GERMAN
BY CATHERINE WINKWORTH

Imagine the awe felt by the shepherds,
as they received the wonderful news.

The heavens declare the glory of God;
the skies proclaim the work of his hands.

PSALM 19:1

(Even without an angel chorus, the night sky inspires reverence.)

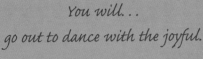

You will. . .
go out to dance with the joyful.

JEREMIAH 31:4

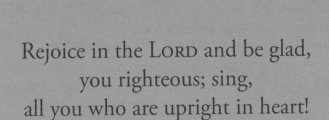

Rejoice in the LORD and be glad,
you righteous; sing,
all you who are upright in heart!

PSALM 32:11

First Snowfall

Those of us who live in the Northern Hemisphere tend to associate Christmas with winter and snow, even if we live in a sunny climate where snow is a rarity. My family was no exception.

Growing up in Southern California, I had seen snow on mountaintops and occasionally played in half-melted snowbanks when the family vacationed in colder areas. I had even seen snow in my own yard—just once. In January of 1949 about half an inch of the white stuff came down during the night. All the kids in the neighborhood were out playing at an hour when their parents were usually trying to get them up for school. We gathered up enough from our large yard to make a very small snowman. We thought there should be a holiday declared, but Mama made us go to school anyway. It was all melted by the time we came home. So I had seen snow but never watched it fall.

My two young sons and I had recently moved to the Seattle area, far from family and friends. The boys hoped for snow, but new acquaintances told us that a wet Christmas was more likely than a white one. It had been raining almost continuously since we arrived in late September, or so it seemed. Thanksgiving had been soggy, and Christmas would probably be the same.

Our budget was tight. I was grateful to be earning enough to pay for

rent, day care, and other necessities. We did what we could to save a few pennies: turned down the thermostat and wore sweaters in the house, turned off lights not in use, used hot water sparingly.

I was cleaning the kitchen after dinner while the boys colored pictures at the table, so we could get by with one light. Suddenly they glanced out the window and squealed, "Snow! It's snowing!" Laughing and yelling, they dashed out the front door, leaving it wide open. I ran after them to reprimand them for letting the heat out of the house.

Outside was an enchanted world. I had always wondered what it would be like to be inside one of those little glass snow globes. Now I knew. Housework and electric bills were forgotten as we twirled and danced, arms outstretched, faces turned up, laughing for pure joy as the soft flakes tumbled down.

But the glory kept shining and bright in my eyes,
And the stars going round in my head.

ROBERT LOUIS STEVENSON, 1850–1894
"ESCAPE AT BEDTIME," *A CHILD'S GARDEN OF VERSES*

It makes no difference whether
we are "poor as church mice" or as wealthy as kings.
The joy of Christmas is for all, whatever our circumstances.

A Make-Do Christmas

Christmas was coming soon. Annie and her two young sons, ages four and six, were far from home and family. Money was scarce. She could manage some sort of gift for each boy, and some candy for the stockings, but there would be no tree and no big family get-together for Christmas dinner.

"Dear Lord," she prayed. "You've done so much for us already. You led us to this safe place, found me a job, and gave us this cozy little house to live in. We have clothes to wear and enough to eat. You've met all our needs. I hate to ask for more. It's not money I need or lots of things, but please show me how to make this Christmas special for my boys."

She continued to kneel in silence, willing her mind to be still. After a few minutes, she began to mentally take stock of her assets. There

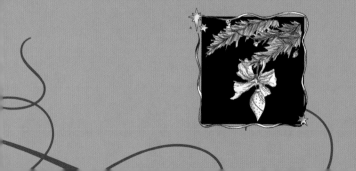

was the small box of ornaments her mother had given her, mostly things that she had purchased herself or made as a child. There was a box of craft supplies: a little construction paper, glue, some leftover paints from a paint-by-numbers project, and various odds and ends. There were the crèche figures, the ones the boys called the Jesus people. She had bought them piecemeal from the dime store with her baby-sitting earnings as a teenager. Each of the little plaster and papier-machè figurines had cost her nearly an hour's labor.

The little people were getting scratched and battered. The boys weren't supposed to touch them, but of course they had. One of the kings had a broken nose, and several of the sheep were missing a leg or two. Maybe they could touch them up with the paints! The boys would like that. They loved any sort of artwork and were already showing signs of talent.

Now she remembered a story she had read, about a visitor to Japan. His friends surprised him on Christmas Eve with a little tree made of evergreen cuttings wired to a frame. It was decorated with folded paper ornaments. *The juniper bushes in the front yard could do with a little pruning,* she thought. And there was some wire in the crafts box. She tiptoed down the stairs and out the front door, pruning shears in hand.

The boys were delighted with the makeshift tree. They decorated it with popcorn strings, paper chains, and Japanese cranes folded from the Sunday comics. Under the tree went two mysterious boxes, wrapped in brown paper, that had come by mail from Annie's family. They hung Christmas cards on the wall and taped cutout paper snowflakes on the windows.

The food budget somehow stretched to include a whole chicken that could be stuffed and baked for Christmas dinner. There were a few yams and a bag of cranberries. The boys were fascinated, watching the cranberries pop as they cooked into sauce. They baked cookies and an apple pie.

The day before Christmas Eve, Annie set out the "Jesus people" and the leftover paints. She put a Christmas record on the record player, and the three of them had a wonderful time making the little figurines look new again. They couldn't fix the lambs' broken legs, but a pile of pine needle "straw" hid the defects.

On Christmas Eve, the boys hung their stockings over a make-believe fireplace they had made of brown wrapping paper taped to the wall. In the morning, they had a sumptuous breakfast of applesauce muffins with raisins and scrambled eggs. Knowing the applesauce for the muffins had come from the windfall apples they had gathered and canned made them taste even better.

Annie read the Christmas story from the Bible before they opened their gifts. While the boys played happily with their new toys, she prepared the Christmas feast. It was truly a glorious Christmas.

Christmas brings hope.
It is a time of new beginnings.
With childlike faith,
we trust that all will be well.

The Birthday of a King

In the little village of Bethlehem,
There lay a Child one day;
And the sky was bright with a holy light
O'er the place where Jesus lay.

Alleluia! O how the angels sang.
Alleluia! How it rang!
And the sky was bright with a holy light
'Twas the birthday of a King.

WILLIAM H. NEIDLINGER, 1890

Happy Birthday, Jesus!

In the Northern Hemisphere, we celebrate Christmas in winter. In the Southern Hemisphere, it comes in summer. Whatever the weather or time of year, let us remember that Jesus is "the reason for the season," and that Christmas is a season of the heart.

But the Christmas bells keep ringing.
Joyous angel choirs are singing,
And the message that they're bringing
Speaks of kindness, love, and cheer.

If you look beyond the trappings,
All the tinsel, toys, and wrappings,
You will find a core of happiness
To last throughout the year.

JANICE LEWIS CLARK,
"CHRISTMAS PREPARATION," 1996

365 Birthdays a Year

Kathy and her mother were decorating for Christmas. As she carefully unwrapped the tissue paper from the manger scene figures, Kathy said, "I wish we could leave them up all year. Why is Christmas always over so soon?"

"It doesn't have to be over," said Mother. "We put the decorations away to keep them special for Jesus' birthday celebration. Sometimes when you see the same things every day, you get so used to them that you don't really notice them anymore. When we put them away for a while, they seem new again. But you can always keep Christmas in your heart."

"How do I do that?" asked Kathy.

"Do you remember what Pastor said about birthday presents for Jesus?"

"Sure," said Kathy. "Jesus said that whatever we do in love for other people is like a gift to Him. That's why we give each other presents on Christmas. But we can't give piles of presents every day."

"No," said Mother, "but I don't think Jesus was talking about giving things. I think He meant to give ourselves. . .doing things to help other people. If you keep your eyes and ears and your heart open, you'll find lots of ways to give. Besides, we don't really know what day is Jesus' birthday. The Bible doesn't say; it could be today or tomorrow or many months away. We just chose a day to celebrate."

"Really?" said Kathy. "So any day of the year could really be Christmas, and we can give Jesus presents every day?"

"That's right," said Mother.

"But why doesn't the Bible say when Jesus was born? And why did people choose December 25?"

"Well," said Mother, "the early Christians didn't celebrate birthdays, so they didn't keep a record of the day. The Roman church chose December 25 over sixteen hundred years ago; the Eastern church chose January 6. No one knows for certain why those days were chosen, but it probably has to do with the winter solstice."

"What's a solstice?"

"Solstice comes from old words meaning *the sun stands still*. Have you noticed the days are longer in summer than in winter? The longest day is near the end of June. After that the days grow shorter, until the winter solstice in December. The ancient people who worshipped the sun celebrated the winter solstice because it meant the light was starting to come back. It was a very holy day for them.

"Even when many of those people became Christians, they didn't want to give up their traditional celebrations. They thought the solstice would be a good time to celebrate the coming of the Son of God and the light He brought to the world."

Just then the doorbell rang. It was Mrs. Jones from next door, wanting to know if Kathy could watch little Tommy while she went to the store.

"Please, may I?" asked Kathy. "It will be my birthday present to Jesus for today. I'll have to think of another one for tomorrow. I want to give Him something every day of the year."

JANICE LEWIS CLARK, DECEMBER 1996

Come, Lord Jesus.

Be our guest.
Join our celebration.

We've decorated our homes
and our cities for You.

We've prepared a feast.

We greet You with
songs and dancing.

We bring You our
most precious gifts.

Come, Messiah, come.

There's a Song in the Air

There's a song in the air! There's a star in the sky!
There's a mother's deep prayer and a baby's low cry!
And the star rains its fire while the beautiful sing,
For the manger of Bethlehem cradles a King!

There's a tumult of joy o'er the wonderful birth,
For the virgin's sweet Boy is the Lord of the earth.
Ay! the star rains its fire while the beautiful sing,
For the manger of Bethlehem cradles a King!

JOSIAH G. HOLLAND, 1872

Let us rejoice with the shepherds,

with the angels, with the wise men.

The kings of this earth delight

in wealth and power,

but the King of the world

brings peace and joy to the meek and lowly.

All He asks in return is that we love Him

and share that love with our neighbors.

All who joy would win
Must share it,
Happiness was born a twin.

GEORGE GORDON NOEL BYRON, 1788–1824

"A new command I give you:
Love one another. As I have loved you,
so you must love one another."

JOHN 13:34

And now these three remain:
faith, hope and love. But the greatest of these is love.

1 CORINTHIANS 13:13

Joy to the World

Joy to the world, the Lord is come!
Let earth receive her King;
Let every heart prepare Him room,
And heaven and nature sing,
And heaven and nature sing,
And heaven, and heaven,
   and nature sing.

Joy to the world, the Savior reigns!
Let men their songs employ;
While fields and floods, rocks, hills and plains
Repeat the sounding joy,
Repeat the sounding joy,
Repeat, repeat, the sounding joy.

ISAAC WATTS, THE PSALMS OF DAVID, 1719

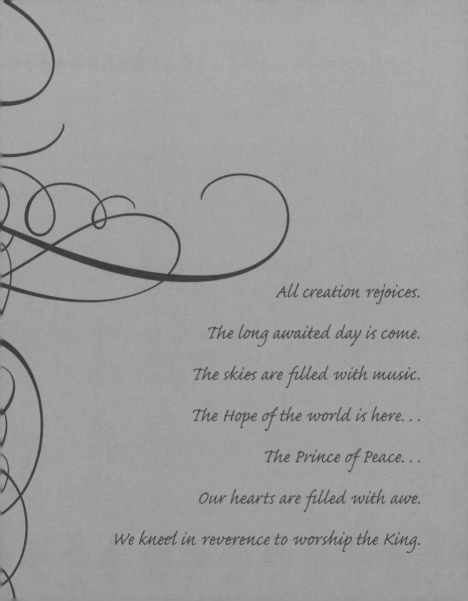

All creation rejoices.

The long awaited day is come.

The skies are filled with music.

The Hope of the world is here. . .

The Prince of Peace. . .

Our hearts are filled with awe.

We kneel in reverence to worship the King.

Angels from the Realms of Glory

Angels from the realms of glory,
Wing your flight o'er all the earth;
Ye who sang creation's story
Now proclaim Messiah's birth.

Come and worship, come and worship
Worship Christ, the newborn King.

Though an Infant now we view Him,
He shall fill His Father's throne,
Gather all the nations to Him;
Every knee shall then bow down:

Come and worship, come and worship
Worship Christ, the newborn King.

JAMES MONTGOMERY SHEFFIELD, 1816

Bright and Joyful Is the Morn

Bright and joyful is the morn,
For to us a Child is born;
From the highest realms of heaven,
Unto us a Son is given.

On His shoulders He shall bear
Power and majesty, and wear
On His vesture and His thigh,
Names most awful, names most high.

Wonderful in counsel be,
Christ, the incarnate Deity;
Sire of ages, ne'er to cease,
King of kings, and Prince of peace.

Come and worship at His feet;
Yield to Him the homage meet;
From the manger to the throne,
Homage due to God alone.

JAMES MONTGOMERY, 1771–1854

"For God so loved the world that he gave his one and only Son, that whoever believes in him shall not perish but have eternal life. For God did not send his Son into the world to condemn the world, but to save the world through him."

JOHN 3:16–17

For to us a child is born,
to us a son is given.

ISAIAH 9:6

"This will be a sign to you:
You will find a baby
wrapped in cloths and lying in a manger."

LUKE 2:12

~

There was, the story says, no room at the inn.
But there is room in my heart. Come, Lord Jesus,
and abide with me always.

Empty Manger

Christmas is a time for children,
All the presents and the lights,
The little baby in the manger
Is such a charming sight.
Lying there so sweet and helpless
In His little bed of straw,
But He's not a little baby
In a manger anymore.
Jesus left the manger,
He grew up and went to work,
Tending His daddy's business like a good son,
Teaching, preaching, searching for the lost ones.
We need to remember
As we celebrate His birth,
That the babe grew up to be the man
Who came to save the earth.

Everybody loves a baby
He's so innocent and small,
You don't expect a babe to lead you
Or do anything at all.
Maybe someday in the future
He'll help you if He can,
Well, if you want the victory now
You need to know the man.
Jesus left the manger
And He's working still today,
Calling on you to join the great adventure
Come and follow anywhere He leads you.
Honor, love, and serve Him
As you give Him all you're worth,
For the babe grew up to be the man
Who came to save the earth.

JANICE LEWIS CLARK, 1998

Christmas is a time of miracles.
To truly keep Christmas in our hearts is to
make room for the Child whose birth we celebrate,
to open ourselves to love, to open our eyes
to the wonders that have been
there all along, unseen.

. . .and it was always said of him, that he knew how to keep Christmas well, if any man alive possessed the knowledge. May that be truly said of us, and all of us! And so, as Tiny Tim observed, "God Bless Us, Every One!"

CHARLES DICKENS, 1812–1870, *A CHRISTMAS CAROL*

Benediction

May peace be with this household
And all who dwell within.
May gracious
hospitality
And natural
generosity
Be recompensed in measure full
And want no foothold win.
May laughter always flourish here
And sorrows comfort find.
May love and kindness banish pain
May every loss be turned to gain
Let joy o'erflowing fill each day
And night leave cares behind.

JANICE LEWIS CLARK, 1995

Merry Christmas...

And a Joyous New Year.